# WILL&KATE

## FAIRY-TALE ROMANCE

Publisher and Creative Director: Nick Wells
Project Editor: Polly Prior
Picture Research: Laura Zats
Layout Design: Jane Ashley
Art Director: Mike Spender
Digital Design and Production: Chris Herbert

Special thanks to: Cat Taylor, Stephen Feather, Dawn Laker, Laura Bulbeck and Karen Fitzpatrick

**FLAME TREE PUBLISHING**
Crabtree Hall, Crabtree Lane
Fulham, London SW6 6TY
United Kingdom

www.flametreepublishing.com

First published 2012

12 14 16 15 13
3 5 7 9 10 8 6 4 2

Flame Tree is part of Flame Tree Publishing Ltd

© 2012 Flame Tree Publishing Ltd

A CIP record for this book is available from the British Library upon request.

ISBN 978-0-85775-372-4

Printed in China

# WILL&KATE

## FAIRY-TALE ROMANCE

ALICE HUDSON

FOREWORD BY JOE LITTLE, *MAJESTY* MAGAZINE

**FLAME TREE
PUBLISHING**

# Contents

# Foreword

**When, on 16 November 2010,** it was finally announced that HRH Prince William of Wales and Miss Catherine Middleton were to marry, the next edition of *Majesty* magazine was about to go to press. For the first – and probably only – time in my career I had to instruct the printers to 'hold the front page' so that I could run with a picture of the newly-engaged couple.

I soon started to receive telephone calls from media organisations around the globe, eager for a comment on the breaking news. At the time, neither I nor my fellow royal correspondents could have guessed what an impact the William and Kate love story would have on people, not just in the following days and weeks but for the next six months too; we had never experienced anything quite like it. And yet why wouldn't the world be interested in a young, attractive couple, particularly when he'd topped the 'Most Eligible Bachelor' lists for so long?

It therefore came as no surprise to be told that an estimated two billion people had watched the 'Wedding of the Century' on television or by other means. But the fascination with the Duke and Duchess of Cambridge continues: their tour of Canada last summer was an incredible success, they were feted by Hollywood A-listers during a working weekend in Los Angeles and back at home every time an item from Kate's high-street wardrobe is identified by fashionistas it sells out immediately.

William and Kate must take much of the credit for the soaring popularity of the British royal family right now. Their relaxed, no-nonsense approach to the way they live their lives has won them many new admirers, who until now had regarded the House of Windsor as posh, privileged and past its sell-by date.

**Joe Little**
Managing Editor, Majesty Magazine

# A Fairy-Tale Romance

**Second in line to the British throne** by blue-blooded birthright, HRH Prince William has long been the subject of girlish princess fantasies the world over. On 29 April 2011, one of the world's most eligible bachelors finally became officially spoken for. After a nine-year courtship, Catherine (Kate) Middleton – stylish, accessibly beautiful and middle class – finally married her prince. Catherine, the Duchess of Cambridge as she is now known, will one day become Queen Consort, providing hubby William takes the throne as expected.

The first 'commoner' with no aristocratic titles to marry into the British Royal Family in 350 years, Kate's fairy-tale wedding was a global news event of epic proportions – attracting up to two billion viewers worldwide. Across the UK, flag-bearing masses whipped themselves into an all-out wedding frenzy, while an adoring public in the hundreds of thousands happily thronged London's streets. It was a day to go down in history.

## A Popular Pair

William and Kate have long enjoyed the approval of each other's families. The public seem to think it a good match too, judging by the thousands of wedding celebrations –

'He'll be thrilled if she's a hit with the public. He's not like his father in this respect. Nothing would please him more than to find people surging past him so that they can get a good look at Kate.'

*A Palace aide*

'We all think he is wonderful
and we are extremely fond of him.
They make a lovely couple,
they are great fun to be with, and
we've had a lot of laughs together.'

*Michael Middleton, speaking following*

*the engagement announcement*

*'There's been a lot of speculation about every single girl I'm with and it actually does quite irritate me after a while, more so because it's a complete pain for the girls.'*

*Prince William*

complete with bunting – held worldwide in their honour. Glamorous, yet down to earth, pretty, yet serious-minded, Kate is perceived as an excellent match for William – a self-described 'country boy at heart' who juggles royal commitments with a full-time job as a Royal Air Force (RAF) rescue helicopter pilot.

Kate's modest style, natural poise, easy charm, intelligence and, above all, unrelenting discretion, are named by royal watchers as traits making her an appropriate choice for a future king. Their relationship and nuptials have helped revive positive press for a monarchy marred by scandal; rejuvenating a family long considered overly stuffy and out of touch. Young, glamorous, rich and royal – Will and Kate would appear to have it all.

## Media Spotlight

Prince William grew up in the media spotlight. While naturally shy, he quickly became accustomed to the attention that was a given for members of 'The Firm'. During his formative years, the sensitive youngster became a first-hand witness to his mother's harassment by the paparazzi, as she became increasingly hounded, right up until the night of her tragic death. Following the tragedy, the media would remain a source of extreme tension for William for many years. To this day, he and Kate fiercely guard their privacy.

In contrast, Kate enjoyed a normal childhood – sans cameras. Yet her life was transformed overnight the moment she was linked to the Prince. As the relationship progressed, the royal girlfriend and her family were forced to endure more and more intrusion. Will has expressed frustration in public several times. It can be argued, however, that Kate's long relationship with Will at least gave her plenty of time to get used to dealing with the media onslaught that is part and parcel of being high profile royalty.

## Royal Chemistry

Kate and Will's relationship has not been without its ups and downs. Yet the attraction, chemistry and mutual respect between the couple has always been evident during public appearances. They share a passion for sport, both playing and spectating, and delighted crowds by turning up as newlyweds to cheer on Murray play at Wimbledon.

According to Katie Nicholl, author of *The Making of a Royal Romance*, William is stubborn, yet Kate 'has this incredible ability to read how he's feeling …' She continues, 'She is intuitive, she gets William in a way no one else does.' Having endured the trauma of his parents' highly sensational divorce in the public eye, William needed considerable time to ensure his commitment would last a lifetime. 'She knew he needed space and time,' says Nicholl. 'She stepped back and gave it to him.'

'I don't deliberately select my friends because of their background. If I enjoy someone's company, then that's all that counts. I have many different friends who aren't from the same background as me and we get on really well – it's brilliant.'

Prince William

'All these questions about do you want to be King? It's not a question about wanting to be, it's something I was born into and it's my duty ... Wanting is not the right word. But those stories about me not wanting to be King are all wrong.'

*Prince William as a teenager*

# The Young Prince

**William Arthur Philip Louis Windsor** was born at 9.03 pm on 21 June 1982 at St Mary's Hospital in Paddington, London. The baby prince weighed in at 7lb 1½ oz, the first born of Charles, the Prince of Wales, and his wife, Diana, Princess of Wales, who was only 20 years old at the time of his birth.

## Blue Blood

William's blue blood flows strong. His mother Diana, although not born into royalty, was nonetheless aristocratic, the daughter of Viscount and Viscountess Althorp of the Spencer clan, one of the UK's oldest and most noted families. Diana's wedding to Prince Charles was viewed by an estimated 750 million people. A further 600,000 people lined London's streets from Buckingham Palace to St Paul's Cathedral, where the couple famously exchanged vows. As the first-born male, second in line to the throne, William grew up with the knowledge he was destined one day to be King. Although his official title from birth was 'His Royal Highness Prince William of Wales', the prince was affectionately called 'Wombat' by his parents as a tot, or 'Wills', the name soon adopted by the press. He has always expressed a desire to be called just 'William'.

## A Mother's Influence

Prince William was 15 years old when his mother died in a Paris car crash on 31 August 1997. The speeding car she was a passenger in was being pursued by paparazzi at the time of the crash. William had always enjoyed a particularly close bond with his mother. He inherited more than her blond locks and bashful, endearing smile – the pair sharing similar sensitive, charitable and down-to-earth natures.

Remembered as a devoted mother who made sure both William and his younger brother, Harry, were exposed to a wider range of experiences than is usual for royal children, Diana famously took them on trips to Walt Disney World and McDonalds. She indulged them with video games while broadening their minds by taking them to AIDS clinics and homeless shelters. Very 'hands on', lacking the traditional stuffiness common in the Royal Family, Diana rarely deferred to her husband, or his family, when it came to decisions such as where to send her boys to school. The story about when William, aged seven, said he wanted to be a policeman when he grew up so he could 'protect' his mother is a touching one. It was little brother Harry who allegedly instantly responded: 'Oh, no you can't. You've got to be King.'

## Education of a Prince

William kicked off his education, aged three, at Mrs Mynor's Nursery School in West London. While there, he performed in a nursery school play, even singing a musical solo. Aged

*'Losing a close family member is one of the hardest experiences that anyone can endure. Never being able to say the word "mummy" again in your life sounds like a small thing. However, for many, including me, it's now really just a word – hollow and evoking memories.'*

*William speaking out for the first time about his mother's death*

four, he graduated to the equally posh Wetherby School. Both Charles and Diana took part in parents' races at the annual sports day. William himself showed an early passion for sports. A natural in the water, aged seven he won a trophy for 'best swimming style'.

*'I like to be in control of my life because I have so many people around me, I can get pulled in one direction, and then the other… I could actually lose my identity.'*

*Prince William*

*'William is a country boy. His mother used to ring me up and say, "William is like a caged lion in London. Can he come and spend the day with your family?"'*

*Lady Annabel Goldsmith*

In 1990, William began the first of five years at Ludgrove School in Berkshire, where he kept swimming while taking up football, basketball, clay pigeon shooting and cross-country running. William broke royal tradition to attend Eton College. There, he studied geography, biology and art history. Always extremely popular among his peers, the talented and intelligent teen captained his house football team, took up water polo and achieved 12 GCSEs and three A Levels. Before university, he took a 'gap' year. During this time, he taught children in Chile, took part in British Army training exercises in Belize, worked on British dairy farms and visited countries in Africa.

*'He loves informality and wants to be treated like everyone else. He once asked a teacher [at Eton] who addressed him as Prince William to "drop the name"'.*

*A source at Eton*

# There's Something About The Girl

**Catherine Elizabeth Middleton** was born on 9 January 1982. She grew up with an ordinary name in an ordinary village, Bucklebury, in Berkshire, England. Catherine's parents had no aristocratic links – descended from coal miners and clergymen. Her father, a former flight dispatcher, had met her mother, an air hostess, while the pair were working for British Airways. By the time Kate was five, her parents had left their frequent flyer days behind them to set up a successful party supplies business – it is now a £30 million operation.

So while 'Kate', as she was known, was no blue blood, she, sister Pippa and brother James certainly enjoyed a very comfortable upbringing. One popular story told by locals in Kate's local area tells of the pleasure her grandmother, who died in 2006, would have got from Kate's wedding. A coal miner's granddaughter, she was allegedly known as 'Lady Dorothy' by some relatives, as she was fanatical about keeping up appearances and 'wanted to be the top brick in the chimney'.

*'Those people who were so recently sneering at her background, and nicknaming her "Waity Katie", will soon be lost in admiration of her poise and professionalism.'*

Historian Andrew Roberts

## School Days

Catherine began her education abroad, at an English language nursery school in Jordan, where her parents were temporarily based while still employed by British Airways.

Upon their return to Berkshire, Kate was enrolled at co-educational preparatory school St Andrew's, in the nearby village of Pangbourne, which set her parents back a cool £13,000 a year in fees. Determined to offer their daughter the best possible education, they then sent her on to Downe House in Cold Ash, near Newbury, where fees are around £10,000 per term. Kate was a day girl at the girls' boarding school, putting her in the minority. By all accounts, she did not enjoy the place and, after just two terms, she upped and left for Marlborough College.

*'I was quite nervous about meeting William's father but he was very, very welcoming and very friendly.'*

*Kate Middleton*

According to some media reports, Kate was bullied relentlessly at Downe by cliquey, bitchy girls, who saw her as too 'skinny', 'nice' and 'meek'. Kate's former headmistress at Downe was forced to insist there was no 'serious' harassment, although she admitted the 'catty' atmosphere and classroom pranks could have left young Kate feeling 'like a fish out of water'. At Marlborough, Kate put any previous troubles behind her, becoming a successful all-rounder and school prefect.

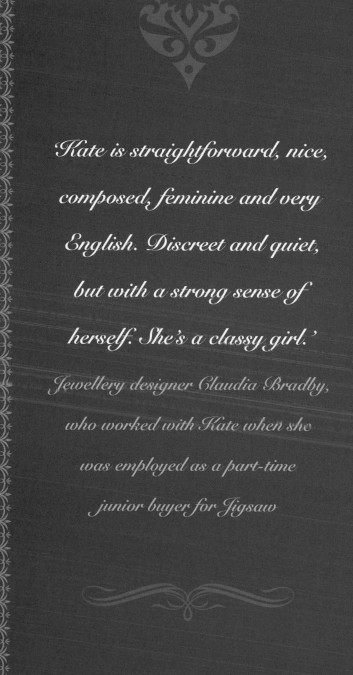

*'Kate is straightforward, nice, composed, feminine and very English. Discreet and quiet, but with a strong sense of herself. She's a classy girl.'*

*Jewellery designer Claudia Bradby, who worked with Kate when she was employed as a part-time junior buyer for Jigsaw*

> *'She's stunning. She's really, really good-looking. She just seemed to be very natural. She had that natural beauty. She still does, but at that time, we didn't know who she was and she did stand out, yeah.'*
>
> *Sophie Butler, Kate's hairdresser while she was studying*

A popular rumour says Kate entertained royal fantasies while at boarding school, pinning a poster of William – the heartthrob prince – on her wall. While Kate rarely adds to media speculation, this is one story she has laughingly denied. 'He wishes,' she said at the official engagement interview. 'I had the Levi's guy on my wall, not a picture of William.'

> *'He's lucky to be going out with me.'*
>
> *Kate Middleton*

## Interests and Strengths

As well as being intelligent and studious, Kate has always been a natural sportswoman. As a child, she relished ski holidays with the family, while competing successfully in a wide range of school sports, including athletics, tennis, field hockey and netball. As if that was not enough, Kate, a former Girl Guide, also excelled culturally. She once played Eliza Doolittle in *My Fair Lady*, learned ballet and tap dancing and was a skilled flautist and singer. According to *Hello* magazine, school pals called her 'a kind-hearted and sensible soul who rarely caused upset among her peers'.

# University Romance

**Brian Lang, the ex-principal** of St Andrews University, said at the graduation of William and Kate in June 2005, 'You'll have made lifelong friends. Not only that, and I say this every year to every group of the new St Andrews graduates: you may have met your husband or wife. Our title as the top matchmaking university in Britain is at stake.' Truer words could not have been spoken for two particular people.

## St Andrews

Fresh from his adventurous gap year, William enrolled at the University of St Andrews in Fife, Scotland. The news a Royal would be among the freshers reportedly caused an influx of last-minute applications to study there – the majority from female students. Kate Middleton can hardly have imagined the huge consequences her own decision to study at St Andrews would have. Placed in the same school residence as HRH, Kate has since admitted she 'went red and sort of scuttled off' the first time she was introduced to her famous classmate. However, the pair soon became good buddies. As William has described it, they enjoyed a 'good giggle and lots of fun' together at Saint Salvator's, known as 'Sallies' – the hall of residence they both bunked down in.

# First Meeting

Exactly when the two hooked up is not publicly known, but William has claimed when they moved in together at the beginning of their second year, it was purely as friends and flatmates. 'We were friends for over a year first and it just sort of blossomed from then on,' the Prince has explained. He has called their friendship a 'good foundation' for the relationship. 'I do generally believe now that being friends with one another is a massive advantage.'

One popular theory is that William was awakened to Kate's charms when he saw her strutting down the catwalk for a student fashion show, DON'T WALK, in 2002, wearing a sheer (now famous) dress that left little to the imagination. Once he had his eye firmly on the prize, Will went all out to woo his girl.

'When I was trying to impress Kate, I was trying to cook these amazing fancy dinners and all that would happen was I'd burn something. Or something would overspill, or something would catch on fire,' he recounted later. 'She'd be sitting in the background just trying to help and basically taking control of the whole situation.'

## Just Good Friends

While William has admitted his housemate romance with Kate at first bemused their friends, it was hardly surprising the two found common ground, despite her middle-class upbringing and his royal one. Their relationship has always been based on friendship and shared interests. Both began university majoring in art history, although William later changed his major to geography, a decision Kate is said to have advised him on. Both did well at their studies and were popular with their peers, although they also loved a good night out dancing, balanced with enough studying to ensure they made their respective families proud. William and Kate both earned Master of Arts degrees, with upper second-class honours; William in geography and Kate in History of Art.

While at university, Prince William represented the Scottish national universities' water polo team at the Celtic Nations tournament in 2004, while Kate kept her love of sports up too, running and rowing among her favourites. 'We had a really good laugh, and then, things happened,' was how Prince William would later explain the natural progression of the relationship.

'When I first met Kate, I knew there was something very special about her. I knew there was possibly something that I wanted to explore there.'

Prince William

*'I first met her at Peter and Autumn's wedding and it was in amongst a lot of other guests and she was very friendly.'*

*Kate on meeting the Queen.*

## Media Scrutiny

Any girlfriend of William's was always going to come under intense media scrutiny. So while rumours of the relationship circulated for years, the two held off confirming they were a couple until 2004, following a March ski trip in Klosters, Switzerland, with Harry and Charles, where they were pictured together looking cosy. The couple were protected from press intrusion to a large degree at St Andrews due to a 'gentleman's agreement' between newspaper editors and the Royal household. Will was known as 'Steve' by other students to avoid any journalists overhearing and realizing his identity.

*'She's got a really naughty sense of humour which helps me, as I've got a really dirty sense of humour.'*

*William on Kate*

The Prince desperately wanted to protect his girlfriend from the tabloid scrutiny that had plagued his mother. While not wanting to shirk his own royal duties and responsibilities, Prince William has always maintained that: 'What I do with my private life is really between me and myself, basically.'

'They could go down to the beach, they could come for drinks here. They could just behave like a normal couple'.

*Justin Hughes, ex-owner of*

MA BELLS, *a St Andrews*

*haunt of the couple*

# Finding Themselves

**While at St Andrews**, the media had kept their promise not to hound the couple. Once Kate and Will graduated and headed to the capital, stress-free nights out with friends became nearly impossible, while pressure began to mount from all sides. Intense speculation about a forthcoming engagement grew to the extent where one hasty company even produced a range of celebratory cups and plates. There would be no rushing the couple, however. Painfully aware of the outcome of his parents' marriage – which eventually ended in divorce in 1996 – William was determined history would not repeat itself. His desire to protect Kate was coupled with a determination to concentrate on his military career and a refusal to be pushed into marriage. Tough times were ahead for the high-profile lovers.

## Careers

William wasted no time throwing himself into military training. He began his career as an officer cadet at the Royal Military Academy at Sandhurst, joining younger brother Harry. After passing out in December 2006, he received a commission as 2nd Lieutenant in the Blues and Royals regiment before becoming a troop commander in an armed reconnaissance unit. 'The last thing I want is to be mollycoddled or be wrapped up in cotton wool', he publicly declared. After

> *'I think it's very important that you make your own decision about who you are. Therefore, you're responsible for your actions, so you don't blame other people.'*
>
> Prince William

completing attachments with the Royal Air Force and Royal Navy, William set his sights on becoming an RAF Search and Rescue pilot, a position he still holds today. William's military posts provided periods of relief from the media spotlight; however, Kate, in London, struggled to lead anything like a normal twenty-something life. She secured a job as an accessories buyer for retailer Jigsaw and later joined the family party supplies business. as a photographer. It seemed to the world she was a princess-in-waiting, leading to the media nickname, 'Waity Katie'.

## Media Invasion

Both private people by nature, the young couple grew increasingly frustrated with the constant throngs of paparazzi. As soon as the couple left Scotland, the media firestorm that had been quietly growing really started to burn. While the first engagement rumours were false, Kate's status in the family appeared to grow, as in 2006 she was granted her own security detail through the Royal and Diplomatic Protection Department. William naturally resented the increasing intrusion into his girlfriend's every move – and she was certainly no fan of the constant attention. She was even forced to cancel her participation in a charity boat race in 2007 due to security concerns.

On her 25th birthday, Kate was mobbed by a large throng of paparazzi as she tried to leave for work in the morning. The pressure did nothing for the relationship and Kate made it

> 'Well, I think if you really go out with someone for quite a long time you do get to know each other very, very well. You go through the good times, you go through the bad times. You know, both personally, but also within a relationship as well.'
>
> Kate Middleton

clear she would not tolerate it. In 2010, she went as far as suing a news agency that distributed pictures of her playing tennis while on holiday, winning damages of £5,000.

## Break-Up

By 2007, it appeared the fairy tale was over. Following a holiday together in Zermatt, Switzerland, on 14 April the story broke that the two were no longer a couple, although Clarence House would only say 'we don't comment on Prince William's private life'. The exact reasons for the break-up are not known for sure, but that it was ultimately William's decision is common knowledge. The original report in *The Sun* newspaper quoted a 'close friend' as saying that Middleton felt Prince William had not been paying her enough attention and had been spending time with female friends. It was also said that the Prince, aged 24 at the time, felt he was too young to marry. A report in the *Daily Mail* newspaper blamed a desire by royal courtiers not to 'hurry along' a marriage announcement, and Prince William's desire to enjoy his bachelor status within his army career.

## Reunion

The split did not last long. Just two months later, the couple were forced to insist they were 'just good friends' after Middleton attended the 'Concert for Diana' memorial celebration the Princes had organized in honour of their late mother. Kate and William sat two rows apart, but rumours of a reconciliation began to flow nonetheless.

Next, Kate was spotted hunting deer with Prince William at Balmoral, was soon mingling at weddings with him, and supporting him during his RAF wings award ceremony and Order of the Garter presentation. In 2008, Kate even attended the wedding of William's cousin Peter Phillips, while William could not make it. With reports they had decided to give their romance a second chance filling the papers, Kate and William stayed out of the media limelight for as long as possible. They were rarely seen out together at their old haunts. It became obvious that the couple were back together and that the split had only been a short one.

*'I think you can get quite consumed by a relationship when you are younger. I really valued that time for me as well, although I didn't think it at the time.'*

*Kate Middleton on the break-up*

'He did cook for me
at university… always
with a bit of anger if
something went wrong.'

Kate Middleton

> 'She's a fantastic girl,
> she really is. My brother is
> very lucky to have found her
> and she's very lucky to have
> found my brother. I think
> the two of them together
> are a perfect match.'
>
> *HRH Prince Harry*

# Stronger Than Ever

**Back together**, the couple appeared stronger than ever. In late 2007, Kate had resigned from her job at Jigsaw. Working for her parents' company, Party Pieces, meant she had more time to support the Prince on the sidelines at polo matches, take trips with him and attend all manner of royal events. Kate has admitted she 'wasn't very happy' during their separation, but insists she now sees it as something that made her 'a stronger person'. 'You find out things about yourself that maybe you hadn't realized,' she is quoted as saying.

## Engagement

William eventually proposed in 2010, finally putting paid to that 'Waity Katie' moniker. The royal proposal happened on a trip to Kenya. While they elected to keep the exact details of the proposal private, what is known is William picked a quiet moment with his girl on a group trip to pop the question – and according to Kate it was 'very romantic' and a big surprise. In November 2010, Clarence House confirmed that Prince William had proposed to Kate a month earlier, and that the couple were engaged and set to marry. Official photographs were taken, and the couple gave their first interview together, both looking radiantly happy.

*Over the years,*

*William has really looked*

*after me. He's treated*

*me very well as the great,*

*loving boyfriend he is.'*

Kate Middleton

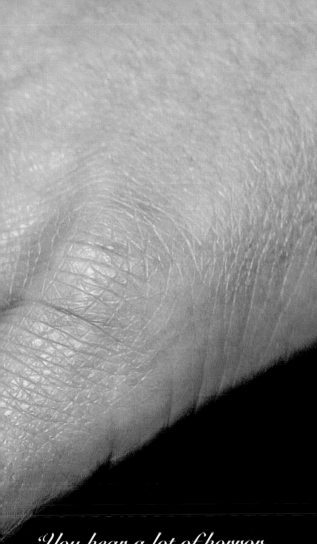

## The Ring

William revealed he was paranoid throughout the Kenyan trip, as he had his late mother's engagement ring hidden in his rucksack. He chose to propose to Kate with the sapphire and diamond ring, which obviously held a particularly special meaning. 'It's my mother's engagement ring so I thought it was quite nice because obviously she's not going to be around to share any of the fun and excitement of it all,' William said in the official engagement interview.

*'I know inside she is nervous. But it doesn't show, and that's what's important. She looks confident.'*

*Arthur Edwards, royal photographer*

Featuring a 12 carat, oval-cut Ceylon sapphire surrounded by 18 diamonds, set in white gold with a narrow yellow gold band, Kate's engagement ring originally cost £28,500 (in 1981) and its value is now estimated up to £250,000. The ring was one of a selection of eight sent to Diana and Charles by Royal Jeweller Garrard.

*'You hear a lot of horror stories about proposing and things going horribly wrong — it went really, really well and I was really pleased when she said yes.'*

*Prince William on proposing*

## Wonderful News

News of the royal engagement made headlines around the world, and sparked happy reactions from all corners. The Queen's representatives tweeted: 'The Queen and The Duke of Edinburgh are absolutely delighted at the news of Prince William and Catherine Middleton's engagement.' The monarch and Prince Philip were full of smiles when seen at an official engagement at the University of Sheffield straight after the announcement was made. Enveloped in a media storm, Kate or 'Catherine' as she was suddenly referred to, opted to read to assembled press from a written family statement, read out by father Michael. He and wife Carole said they were 'absolutely delighted' with the news and had, over the years, got to know Will well. 'We all think he's wonderful and we're extremely fond of him. They make a lovely couple, they are great fun to be with and we've had a lot of laughs together.'

Speaking candidly to a television reporter while on an Arctic trek, HRH Prince Harry appeared overjoyed. When asked what his mother would think, he had this to say: 'She'd be very, very proud that the big day has come – you know we all thought it was never going to happen for him, but it has happened and I think everyone's going to be really proud of him and it's a big deal'. 'It's not just a normal wedding, it's a really big decision for him to bring Kate into the family, there's obviously a huge amount of pressure from the media, from the public perception and everything like that. He's done the right thing, he's waited and he's done it when he's felt right.' Clarence House immediately tweeted,

'During a visit to Poundbury in Dorset, The Prince of Wales said he is "thrilled" at the news of Prince William's engagement'. Charles also later joked, 'They've been practising long enough.' His wife Camilla described the engagement as 'the most brilliant news'.

*'I thought if I ask Kate first, then [Kate's father] can't really say no, so I did it that way round.'*

*Prince William*

'It's quite good news always to outfox the media. But it was a military style operation and my brother and I are proud of how it went.'

*Prince William on his stag do*

# Wedding Plans

**The couple**, the Royal Family and British authorities, particularly the Met Police, had much to think about to ensure what was quickly dubbed 'the wedding of the century' went off without a hitch. Much of the cost of the massive celebration would be to do with security. Anti-terrorism and protection measures to protect the Royal Family and visiting world leaders reportedly cost up to £20 million, and included the services of 5,000 armed police in London on the day, as well as snipers on rooftops. The couple themselves were keen to appear budget conscious, however, considering the economic climate. They insisted on canapés only for their main reception, for instance, and drove to the ceremony in cars, rather than the traditional, and far more costly, carriages.

'It's a big deal. It's not just a normal wedding. It's a really big decision for him to bring Kate into the family.'

*Prince Harry on Prince William's wedding plans*

The Prince enjoyed a stag do, which he managed to keep secret from the media until after the event. Will spent his last weekend as a bachelor at Hartland Abbey in North

Devon, a family mansion of his friend's, where he and a dozen pals even managed a spot of surfing as well as some clay pigeon shooting. Meanwhile, Kate opted to keep things even quieter, celebrating with a 'quiet night in' with a small group of friends.

## When and Where

Their courtship was an untraditionally long 10 years, yet once the engagement was revealed, the Royal Family took just seven days to announce a date and location. What was quickly dubbed 'the wedding of the century' was to take place on Friday 29 April 2011 at Westminster Abbey.

The day was swiftly declared a bank holiday so the nation could watch the spectacle and join in the celebrations. According to a royal aide, the couple had pushed for a Friday during spring to wed. BBC News reported they chose the Abbey for 'its staggering beauty, 1000-year royal history and feeling of intimacy despite its size'. Despite its 2,200 capacity, William's private secretary Jamie Lowther-Pinkerton claimed William thought the Abbey felt 'like a parish church'.

The choice of venue came as no surprise, despite its painful association for William – his mother's funeral was also held at Westminster. The only other venue under serious consideration – and unsurprisingly rejected by the young couple – was St Paul's Cathedral, the site where Diana and Charles had wed. The Queen, the Queen Mother, Princess Margaret, Princess Anne and The Duke of York all married at the Abbey.

*'William and Kate have thoroughly enjoyed the process of creating their special day. They have been responsible for everything from the smallest detail, such as the reception canapés, to the big decisions like the carriages.'*

*A Palace spokesman*

## Doing it Their Way

With only five months until the big day, the young couple had more than enough to keep them occupied. Despite the help of an army of staff, the couple made it clear they would take a hands-on approach when it came to the details.

Kate worked alongside Prince Charles to choose the music. The bride came armed with 'mood boards' when selecting floral arrangements, chose Fiona Cairns to create an eight-tier masterpiece of a wedding cake and was involved in every last wedding detail – even choosing to scent the church with her favourite orange-blossom Jo Malone candles.

William and Kate wanted to make the day as accessible to the public as possible, so wedding coverage was streamed live on YouTube. The Prince's press office also provided a live blog throughout the day.

The couple refused to accept traditional gifts, opting instead for well-wishers to donate to charity. They also went to pains to reassure the public they were aware of the economic climate, insisting on certain less extravagant measures.

## You're Not On The List

The highly coveted invitations were sent out by Royal Mail in mid-February. Close to 1,900 people were lucky enough to

receive 'the golden tickets' which, printed on thick white card, were bevelled, gilded and stamped with EIIR in gold, which was then burnished.

While speculation began to mount immediately as to who would make the cut, an official list was not released until 23 April, when Clarence House confirmed it had invited more than 50 members of the Royal Family and 40 crowned heads from Europe and around the world, including the Prince of Saudi Arabia, the King of Tonga, the Sheik of Kuwait and the Princess of Thailand. Over 60 Prime Ministers and governor generals of countries including Australia and New Zealand, Papua New Guinea and Barbados received the invites. William and Kate chose 250 of their friends to attend, while Kate's parents were allowed a quota of 100. Kate's rumoured ex-boyfriends Rupert Finch and Willem Marx, and William's former flames, Isabella Anstruther-Gough-Calthorpe, Arabella Musgrave, Rose Farquhar and Jecca Craig, also received the royal nod. Notable snubs included Barack and Michelle Obama, and Fergie, the Duchess of York as well as William's cousin Beatrice's boyfriend of five years Dave Clark and Lady Annabel Goldsmith, one of Diana's closest friends.

*'We're like ducks, all calm on the surface, but the little feet are going under the water.'*

*Prince William on wedding preparations*

*'I did the rehearsals the other day and my knees started going, tapping quite nervously, so it's quite a daunting prospect.'*

*Prince William reveals his nerves with four weeks to go*

'We're quite a reserved lot, the British, but when we go for it, we really go for it.'

Prime Minister

David Cameron

# The Big Day

**The wedding itself was a triumph**, with all going according to a very exact plan. By 9.50 am, most of the 1,900 guests were already inside the Abbey for the 11 am service. William and Harry arrived at 10.15 am, The Queen arrived at 10.45 am and Kate was denied the usual bride's indulgence of being late, departing in a Rolls Royce Phantom VI with her father, from the posh Goring Hotel at precisely 10.51 am to get to the Abbey on time.

## Public Party

Prime Minister David Cameron had said he wanted the wedding to be 'a day of national celebration' and that it certainly was. The British public, not to mention the throngs of overseas visitors, embraced the celebratory, flag-waving spirit that swept the nation.

Over 5,000 street parties were held to mark the Royal Wedding throughout the UK and one million people lined the route between Westminster Abbey and Buckingham Palace in London. Hardcore royal fans camped out for days just to get a good spot along the processional route. Expats gathered in pubs around the world, while Kate's hometown celebrated in its own style. London's Clapham Common was turned into a giant camping ground and crowds gathered to watch big screens in

Hyde Park. Over 72 million tuned in to the YouTube Royal Channel. It seemed Royal Wedding mania had swept the land, with even cynics eventually getting caught up in the hype.

## You Are On The List

The congregation began arriving from 8.15 am to 9.45 am, and distinguished guests from 9.50 am; of course, their outfit choices were scrutinized closely live on TV. Victoria Beckham arrived with hubby David – she in surprisingly towering stilettos, considering her heavily pregnant state; he with O.B.E on the wrong lapel. Both looked fabulous.

Guy Ritchie was there, a distant cousin of Kate's, as were Sir Elton John and David Furnish. William's cousin Princess Beatrice stunned the watching throngs with her strange Philip Treacy hat, which immediately drew a myriad of comparisons – was she wearing antlers, an octopus or a loo seat? Treacy had plenty more accessible pieces on show – the milliner had made 36 creations for the big day. Ex-party girl Tara Palmer Tomkinson wore a cobalt-blue Deborah Milner dress, the Queen wore yellow, while the PM's wife, Samantha Cameron, raised eyebrows by not wearing a hat.

## Get Me To The Church On Time

The ceremony was overseen by John Robert Hall, the Dean of Westminster; Rowan Williams the Archbishop of Canterbury

*'Poor Posh – she is trying so hard not to smile because she doesn't like her face when she does but she desperately wants to.'*

*Sports broadcaster Clare Balding on Victoria Beckham*

conducted the marriage ceremony itself, while Richard Chartres, the Bishop of London, gave the sermon. Maple trees had been brought into the Abbey giving it a forest-like feel. A reading was given by the bride's brother James.

It was a long, three-and-a-half minute walk down the aisle to the altar. Kate's incredible composure impressed everybody. Prince William looked resplendent in the red uniform of his honorary rank of Colonel of the Irish Guards. A memorable moment occurred when Harry turned to sneak a peek at the bride. 'She's here,' he said to his nervous brother with a grin. 'Just wait till you see her.'

Catherine chose to omit the word 'obey' from her vows, following in Diana's footsteps. She instead promised to 'love, comfort, honour and keep' Prince William. William also broke with royal tradition by having a best man – brother Harry – instead of a 'supporter' as is the norm.  Four bridesmaids and two pageboys were led by Pippa Middleton, maid of honour, into the Abbey, followed by Catherine and her father.

The Westminster Abbey Choir, the Chapel Royal Choir – of angelic young male voices – and the London Chamber Orchestra provided much of the music, the theme of which was 'Best of British' and which included dramatic hymns 'Greensleeves', 'Jerusalem' and 'Guide Me, O Thou Great Redeemer'. The Central Band of the Royal Air Force provided the fanfare.

*'You just felt a huge great sense of privilege that you were there. It's got the build up of almost of a family wedding, everyone milling around... everybody waving at each other. And then suddenly in comes Prince William and Prince Harry, and suddenly there's a sense of here we are, we are watching history.'*

*Robert Hardman,*
*royal expert and author*

## The Parade

On leaving the Abbey to the pealing of bells, the couple passed through an individually selected guard of honour made up from defence services, to be greeted by loud cheers from the waiting throngs. According to *Vanity Fair*, as the couple climbed into the Queen's 1902 State Landau carriage, drawn by four white horses, Duchess Catherine turned to her husband and said, 'Are you happy?' 'Very,' he replied, taking her hand. 'This is mad. Gosh, the noise.'

The couple returned to Buckingham Palace along the same route that had been taken by those who had departed there prior to the ceremony. It took in Parliament Square, Whitehall, Horse Guards Arch, Horse Guards Parade, Clarence House and The Mall. The newly married couple were escorted by mounted escort of the Life Guard. The weather held, and the crowds continued to cheer as the carriage, followed by a similar carriage containing the rest of the bridal party, then coaches containing the Queen and other Royals, passed.

The next big moment was when the bridal party appeared on the balcony of Buckingham Palace. Applause from the crowded Mall was deafening and Duchess Catherine, as she prefers to now be known, was seen trying to distract one three-year-old bridesmaid who had covered her ears and was looking distressed. The crowd cheered 'kiss, kiss, kiss' and after waving, the couple kissed, ever so briefly, on the lips. William turned to Kate and said: 'Let's give them another one. I love you.' They kissed again, briefly, and by 1.31 pm it was all over, as first the Queen, then the others, retreated inside.

*'Checkmate Kate –*
*you've taken the King.'*

*Words on a banner among the*

*cheering crowds*

'I love where she comes from and who she is. You see them together and they're easy with each other. They look at each other with genuine interest and love. It takes a very special person to step into that world.'

Dame Helen Mirren

## Just Married

As guests thronged in the courtyard of the palace, another break from tradition was about to occur. William hopped in to the driver's seat of his dad's Aston Martin DB6 Volante. The car had been a 21st birthday present from Queen Elizabeth to her son. William drove his new bride the short distance to the London home of Charles and Camilla, Clarence House. Prince Harry had decorated the Aston Martin with a number plate, JU5T WED. The couple were accompanied by a bright yellow RAF search and rescue chopper.

## Private Parties

The wedding became more intimate and exclusive as the day wore on. A lunchtime reception at Buckingham Palace hosted by the Queen saw 650 invited. A team of 21 chefs prepared the 'finger food' fare the couple had insisted on, featuring mini Yorkshire puddings with beef, Cornish crab salad and Scottish smoked salmon. The Pol Roger NV Brut Reserve was flowing, served in crystal flutes, and William spoke well, calling his new wife a 'wonderful girl'.

The evening saw the Queen depart and the next party begin. Kate and William had invited just 300 to this part of the celebration. Guests arrived in blacked-out limos at seven. Kate changed into a strapless white McQueen evening gown, with diamante sash, an angora bolero keeping her warm.

'William spoke very well, but it was Charles who really gave praise to his daughter-in-law. He said they were really lucky to have a daughter like her.'

Dr Robert Acheson, the headmaster of Kate's former primary school

Princesses Beatrice and Eugenie, Zara Phillips and fiancé Mike Tindall, and Peter Phillips and wife Autumn were in attendance, as was Pippa Middleton, in an emerald green evening dress by Alice Temperley. Chelsy Davy, Harry's ex-girlfriend sat next to him, while William's former flame, Jecca Craig, also made the cut. Just before midnight, guests were led into the Throne Room, transformed into a nightclub. The bride and groom took to the floor to a rendition of Elton John's 'Your Song' by Ellie Goulding, whom they had specially requested for the evening. A fireworks display ended the night with a bang at 2.30 am.

## The Honeymoon

Despite news reports that the Duke and Duchess would depart for their honeymoon the day after their wedding, they in fact decided to wait ten days. William went back to work on the Monday after a private weekend together, ensuring a slight cool-down of the media fever, which then allowed the couple to escape more easily when the time came.

The location of the honeymoon was a tightly guarded secret, with not even Kate being let in on the destination. Speculation was rife, fuelled by the knowledge that the Duchess favoured somewhere warm to celebrate the nuptials. South America, Kenya, Necker Island, Mustique or Jordan were hot favourites in the media speculation; however, the couple ultimately flew to a private island in the Seychelles, where they had previously stayed in 2007 on a 'make or break' trip. They flew by private jet from Anglesey to a luxury villa with its own pool and butler service.

'I remember standing in Westminster Abbey thinking "this is unreal". It was like a fairy tale. And all I could think was, "I hope I don't trip over". I didn't realise the enormity of it until much nearer the wedding day. It was a magical experience.'

Kate about her wedding day.

# The Dress

**As for every bride**, selecting the perfect dress was at the top of Kate's wedding priorities. Unlike other brides, she had a global audience of 2 billion to consider, and had her work cut out keeping the design a secret from her beau. The media and bookmakers speculated for months as to who would win the all-important contract, with British fashion houses considered the most likely. Red herrings included the spotting of Kate's mother and sister shopping at Bruce Oldfield. There were even rumours Kate was having up to three dresses made.

The eventual result, by the late Alexander McQueen's successor Sarah Burton, was widely acclaimed and has single-handedly put lace and beading back in bridal fashion. The designer said even her parents did not know about the job until the night before, while seamstresses remained unaware of what they were working on. Pippa Middleton's sleek, sexier, fitted cowl neck maid of honour creation – also by Burton – generated just as much admiration on the day. High street stores scrambled to copy both designs.

*'I think what we wanted to achieve was something that was incredibly beautiful and intricately worked.'*

*Designer Sarah Burton on Kate's gown*

# The Designer

Sarah Burton is creative director at British fashion house Alexander McQueen. Kate's choice of label was particularly poignant as its creator, the extraordinarily talented and celebrated man of the same name, had tragically taken his own life in February 2010. In a video shown to the public at a wedding dress exhibition held at Buckingham Palace, Burton explains Kate had a 'hands-on' approach in assisting with design elements. Kate, Burton said, wanted a gown with 'presence and historical importance' but it also had to have a contemporary feel. 'We wanted to look to the past, but look to the future as well,' Burton said. Burton was named designer of the year in 2011 by influential fashion title *Harper's Bazaar* at its annual Women of the Year awards.

# A Work of Art

The dress featured a Grace Kelly-inspired lace bodice, hand-stitched by seamstresses from the Royal School of Needlework. The cinched waist emphasized the bride's tiny proportions, while the full skirt and 2.7 m (9 ft) train put paid to speculation Kate would go for something simple. Fifty-eight gazar buttons ran from the collar to the waist on the gown, which was priced at a cool £250,000.

According to the designer, the gown had 'an essence of Victorian corsetry', with the cinched waist and a bustle to keep the shape of the dress at the back. However, the dress was cut in a modern way and featured intricate handcrafted long, lace sleeves.

'It was so great to actually keep a secret, especially in this day and age when everyone talks about everything.'

*Dress designer*

*Sarah Burton*

> 'Kate wearing her hair as she has is the death of the straightening iron. It's all about a girl's best friend – the heated roller.'
>
> *Celebrity hair stylist*
>
> *Andrew Barton*

## Jewellery

Despite speculation she would wear flowers in her hair, Kate opted to go with a 1936 Cartier 'halo' tiara. It fitted into the 'something borrowed' category, as it was on loan from the Queen herself, who had received it for her 18th birthday. The Queen had offered three choices of tiara to Kate, who predictably opted for the simplest, most understated piece.

To complement the exquisite tiara, which features 1,000 diamonds, Kate wore a pair of diamond earrings received as a pre-wedding gift from her parents. They featured an acorn design, representing the Middleton family's new coat of arms. Kate's wedding ring is made from Welsh gold, fashioned from a piece the Queen had retrieved from the royal vaults and gifted to William. Prince William chose not to receive a wedding ring at the ceremony.

> 'We backcombed the top to create a foundation for the tiara to sit around, then did a tiny plait in the middle and sewed it on. I've never seen anything like it in my life.'
>
> *Kate's hair stylist James Pryce*

## Down To The Last Detail

Kate's hair was styled in loose curls by James Pryce of Richard Ward Salon. He revealed he spent weeks practising the delicate up-do with a cheap £6.50 tiara from the shop Claire's Accessories. Kate insisted on doing her own make-up, which was typically understated, although the entire bridal party received 'make-up artistry assistance' from Bobbi Brown artist Hannah Martin. Her nails were painted in a mixture of two polishes, a 'barely there' pink and 'sheer beige'. The bridal veil was made of soft ivory silk tulle and stitched with flowers. Kate wore size five-and-a-half, hand-stitched, low stiletto, closed-toe shoes. An 8-tiered traditional fruit cake was cut by the couple at their reception using a ceremonial sword. A special chocolate biscuit cake was also produced to suit William's tastes. Flowers used in the bridal bouquet included sweet William, hyacinth, lily of the valley and myrtle.

*She is so stunningly beautiful, it's so regal, it's such understatement that I think it's just perfection. Everybody is starstruck with her gown.' Harold Tillman, chair of the British Fashion Council*

# Married Life

**Following the wedding**, the royal couple quickly settled into a routine in Anglesey, Wales. Following the Friday wedding ceremony, William even showed up on Monday morning for a normal shift of work as an RAF search and rescue pilot. The couple love the peace and quiet of the country, and by all accounts they have been warmly welcomed into the community, becoming regulars at local pubs, while Kate was quickly invited to join the Wives Club at RAF Valley.

## Normal Life

The Duke and Duchess appear refreshingly down to earth. Despite Prince Charles's offer of a larger staff following the wedding, the couple refused. In the days following the wedding and before the honeymoon, Kate was photographed pushing a grocery trolley across the car park at the local Waitrose in Anglesey. Kate has the assistance of a housekeeper, but insists on doing all the cooking for William herself. She has no 'ladies-in-waiting'. The couple expressed, prior to their wedding, that when it came to official engagements, they wanted 'minimal fuss' and as small an entourage as possible. The royal couple like to keep things as informal and low-key as possible, although for Kate, in particular, born a commoner, life may never feel 'normal' again. She has had to become accustomed to the presence of bodyguards, usually three, in a policy enforced since the day of the engagement.

# A Home of Their Own

The couple's Anglesey farmhouse is rented by the pair for a reported £750 per month. Yet in November 2011, it was announced the Duke and Duchess of Cambridge were set to make Kensington Palace in West London their permanent family home. William and Catherine are expected to move into the late Princess Margaret's former '1A' apartment sometime in 2013, after extensive renovations costing around £1 million are completed.

Currently, when in London, the couple stay at Nottingham Cottage, a two-bedroom dwelling on the Kensington grounds. Moving inside will likely take some getting used to – the residence has 21 rooms over four floors, including a large dining room, drawing room, study, nursery and private, walled garden. The residence will come with staff, likely consisting of at least a butler, housekeeper, valet, chef and chauffeur. The couple are expected to put their own stamp on the place when it comes to style. Empty since the Queen's sister died in 2002, much of the apartment remains painted in Princess Margaret's favourite colours – turquoise and pink.

# Royal Duties

In allowing William to pursue his dream career as a pilot, the Queen has permitted the Duke and Duchess a two-year grace period from full-time royal duties. The couple have not been let off the hook entirely, however. The couple's first public engagement together following their high-profile wedding was an appearance on 10 June 2011 at a gala

'I get quite lazy about cooking because when I come back from work, the last thing I want to do, really, is spend loads of time cooking.'

Prince William

*'No one is going to try to fill my mother's shoes, what she did was fantastic. It's about making your own future and your own destiny and Kate will do a very good job of that.'*

Prince William

dinner for the Absolute Return for Kids (ARK) charity. The couple attended on behalf of the Foundation of Prince William and Prince Harry, which raises money for causes associated with young people around the world.

The following day, Kate watched William in his first Trooping the Colour parade, an annual event held in honour of the Queen's official birthday. On 30 June 2011, the Duke and Duchess departed on their first ever official overseas trip. The nine-day North American tour began in Ottawa, Canada and took in Prince Edward Island, Calgary and California. All eyes were on Kate and she did not disappoint, conducting herself with poise and dignity, appearing happy, stylish and confident.

The couple mingled with Barack and Michelle Obama and Hollywood stars. It was Kate's first time to the States and she was said to be 'beyond excited'. Six months after the wedding, Kate completed her first solo engagement, stepping in for the Prince of Wales at a private dinner for charity In Kind Direct, after Charles was called away at the last minute.

## Charities

Aiding charities is a big part of being a modern Royal, and is something William has long taken part in. Following in his mother's footsteps, he takes a 'hands-on' approach, even spending a night sleeping rough on the street in the name of raising awareness of homelessness. His and Harry's memorial concert for their mother in 2007 raised over £1.2 million for

charities. Choosing which charities to support is one of Kate's main priorities as a new Duchess. William and Kate personally selected 26 charities that had 'particular resonance' with them to benefit from the wedding fund. These included the London Zoo's black rhino project and Beatbullying. The latter is thought to have been included due to Kate's personal experience of being bullied at school, and the charity has said it will ask her to become a patron.

After the couple opened a new centre for children at London's Royal Marsden Hospital, she showed her submissive side; when asked by cancer patient Shirley Carpenter if she would make the hospital one of the charities the couple support, she said: 'We'll have to see – William's in charge.' Kate later made headlines for the long personal letter she sent nine-year-old leukaemia patient Fabian Bate, after promising to read his blog and posting a message on it.

*'I'm just very grateful to Kate Middleton for making looking appropriate really fun again.'*

*Anne Hathaway*

# Queen of Style

**With her tiny waistline**, natural-looking blow-dried locks, radiant complexion and ability to pull off striking colour choices including white, scarlet and emerald, Kate's naturally evolving style is admired across the globe. The Duchess is yet to hire a professional stylist and seemingly does not need to, regularly featuring in 'best dressed' lists, although she is not without critics.

Dame Vivienne Westwood said after her Red label fashion show on 20 February: 'I would have loved to dress Kate Middleton but I'll have to wait until she kind of catches up a bit with style.' While at New York Fashion Week (2011), the local 'fash pack' said Kate followed trends rather than set them. Yet, in what has been dubbed 'The Kate Effect', any item of clothing she is pictured in quickly sells out. Incredibly, the see-through £30 dress that famously caught William's eye in 2002 sold at auction for $125,871 in March 2011.

*'I'm shaking – she's not just one of those pretty people in magazines. She's actually even prettier.'*

*Fan Chiara Guglielmi, on meeting Kate in Canada*

## Becoming an Icon

Kate has always been a naturally stylish dresser. Aside from the sheer dress that caught William's eye at university, the most risqué outfit she has been pictured in is a pair of yellow hot pants and green sequined halter-neck top – and it *was* appropriate, being a roller disco charity event.

Since her engagement was announced, Kate's fashion choices have become increasingly elegant and chic, propelling her to 'style icon' status. A fan of fascinators, cinched waistlines, dainty jewellery and modest hemlines, Kate first began attracting attention in fashion pages in 2006, when *The Daily Telegraph* named her Most Promising Newcomer in its list of style winners and losers. *Tatler* ranked her among 10 style icons in 2007, and since then she has been lauded by a myriad of publications, from *Vanity Fair* to *Vogue,* from *Style.com* to *People.* In 2011, *Harper's Bazaar* named the Duchess 'Britain's Queen of Style' at its Women of the Year Awards.

*She's modern, really modern. She's smart to mix cheap clothes with the likes of Alexander McQueen.'*

*Anna Dello Russo, editor-at-large of* VOGUE *Japan*

## Royal Recycler

Even now she's an official Royal, sensible Kate has no qualms about recycling her outfits, or shopping from high street stores. She was famously photographed on the King's Road in London pre-honeymoon, selecting outfits from Whistles, Banana Republic and Warehouse, and wore a

Top Shop dress at her 25th birthday bash. She also loves Zara, French Connection and LK Bennett. Recycling past outfits fits with her image as a 'people's duchess'.

At a Los Angeles reception, during the couple's recent North American tour, she wore the same green Diane von Fürstenberg dress she had been pictured in at Zara Phillips' pre-wedding bash. During the same tour, the new Royal was also seen in the same J Brand jeans three times and on Canada Day, 1 July, she wore the same white Reiss dress she had chosen for the official engagement pictures.

In June 2011, Kate wore the same Zara dress to a friend's wedding that she had been seen in on a night out in London back in 2007. Entire websites are dedicated to following Kate's every fashion move.

*'I haven't given her any style advice. Why would she need any from me? She never puts a foot wrong. She knows what suits her.'*

*Style guru and Kate's step-sister-in-law Sara Buys, wife of Tom Parker Bowles*

'*No one has really seen princesses except on TV – on TV they are usually stuck up like the evil stepsisters. But she was so sweet and pretty and nice and so was Prince William.*'

*Sneh Chachra, 10, who met the couple in L.A.*

## Best of British

Kate is a champion of British fashion. She makes a patriotic statement almost every time she steps out, her wedding gown by Sara Burton of McQueen being the most obvious example. A designer ranked among the Duchess's favourites is Daniella Helayel, of high-end London label Issa. After Kate chose a navy blue, long sleeve Issa design for her engagement announcement, stocks of the £385 dress sold out within 24 hours.

She is also a big fan of high street brand Reiss: she chose one of their dresses for a meeting with Michelle Obama (the resulting demand saw the Reiss website crash) and a Reiss coat when William received his RAF wings in 2008;

'We'll sort of get over the marriage first and then maybe look at the kids. But, obviously, we want a family so we'll have to start thinking about that.'

*Prince William*

she also wore a white Reiss dress for the official engagement photographs. Other home-grown labels she has famously worn include Burberry, Temperley, Mulberry and Amanda Wakeley, whose couture was also loved by Diana, Princess of Wales. British designers Katherine Hooker, Jenny Packham and Sophie Cranston of Libelula have also benefited from Kate's patronage.

## Royal Patronage

In January 2012, the same month she celebrated her 30th birthday, it was announced that the Duchess of Cambridge had chosen four charitable organizations initially to align herself with. Hundreds of worthy causes had been clamouring to attract the coveted patronage of the glamorous Royal so Kate's decision was, by all accounts, an exceedingly tough one.

Kate's love of art was reflected in her decision to become patron of The National Portrait Gallery. She also chose to support London-based charity, The Art Room, which aims to teach youth life skills to disadvantaged youth through art. Action on Addiction and East Anglia's Children's Hospices (EACH) completed the quartet of charities granted the Royal seal of approval. In addition, 2012 saw Kate begin to volunteer as a Scout leader.

# What Lies Ahead

**One day, they will become King and Queen** of England. Until then, the Duke and Duchess of Cambridge will be expected to keep up a steady stream of public appearances and overseas tours, maintain their charity work and raise a family – after all, a key part of the monarchy is producing an heir. The Duke will continue to serve with the RAF until at least 2013, when his current contract expires. After that, he could leave the RAF and take up royal duties full time, or continue for another three years.

It is rumoured he may serve at least another three-year period, perhaps in Scotland, where the couple first met. A royal aide told the media that the Duke is conscious his pilot training cost £800,000 and wants his career to have been worth the investment. What the couple will want to avoid at all costs is scandal and divorce. If Kate becomes Queen, she will be the first to hold a university degree.

There is genuine public affection for William and Catherine, the Royal Family's golden couple, and will want to wish them well for all that is to come.

*In the busyness of each day, keep our eyes fixed on what is real and important in life, and help us to be generous with our time, love and energy.'*

*From Kate and William's wedding prayer*

*'When you meet them, you don't have to bow and curtsy. You can call them whatever you feel: Your Royal Highness, William and Kate, just as the mood takes you.'*

BAFTA *chairman*

*Duncan Kenworthy*

# Biographies

## Alice Hudson (Author)

From New Zealand, **Alice Hudson** fused twin passions for writing and music while a student, reviewing and interviewing international bands and DJs. She is currently based in London, writing and researching for corporate clients across a wide range of sectors, from health and fitness and financial services, to social media and entertainment.

## Joe Little (Foreword)

**Joe Little** has been managing editor of *Majesty* for 12 years. In that time he has met some weird and wonderful people, and has travelled extensively on royal assignments. Highlights include a fantastic trip to Kuala Lumpur, where he found himself dancing the *poco-poco* with the Queen of Malaysia, and a long weekend in Riyadh, flying on one of the King of Saudi Arabia's private aircraft. Joe's working life is almost as varied as that of Queen Elizabeth II and her family, and occasionally he gets to meet them too.

# Picture Credits